A Chat Between Friends.

How Did You

Get Started Writing?
What Did and Did Not Work For Me.

Kelly J. Stigliano

Apple Butter Publications, 2023

Dedication

The question I get asked the most is how I got started writing. I dedicate this book to those who've asked that question and those who have yet to ask. I don't claim to know everything, but I know what worked for me. If reading this can lead you down a smoother path to your writing mission, or at least help you avoid my mistakes, then I've met my goal!

This is a friendly chat between you and me.

Do you have a burning desire to write? Then you must write! Let's get you started because you have a story that only you can tell.

∞∞∞∞∞∞

Each of you should use whatever gift you have received to serve others, as faithful stewards of God's grace in its various forms. (1 Peter 4:10)

Go now, write it on a tablet for them, inscribe it on a scroll, that for the days to come it may be an everlasting witness. (Isaiah 30:8)

He who was seated on the throne said, "I am making everything new!" Then he said, "Write this down, for these words are trustworthy and true." (Revelation 21:5)

This is what the Lord, the God of Israel, says: "Write in a book all the words I have spoken to you." (Jeremiah 30:2)

Write, therefore, what you have seen, what is now and what will take place later. (Revelation 1:19)

Writing is important!

Contents

Introduction

It burns in your chest like when your heart is on fire for the one you love; like the overwhelming desire to be with that person; it's a pleasant burn. It's a burn that's hard to define, like a scream that is somehow being stifled. You have a message that has to be shared. You have a story to tell.

I'm here to tell you how I fulfilled that burning desire to write, to communicate, to help, to share my passion via the written word. I write nonfiction, but there is much to glean from this book to help with writing fiction, as well.

I don't have all the answers, but I know where to find them. For decades I was a journalist and research is my forte. I've always been honest with my readers and those reaching out to me. The main purpose of this book is to get you where you want to be as a writer, so I won't beat around the bush. I'll admit what I don't know and will tell you who does. Through this, I hope to help you move into the next phase of your writing career or to get started from scratch.

Just to get this out of the way, allow me to vet myself for you. As of this writing, I've been in fifteen compilation books, including three Chicken Soup for the Soul editions, three Guideposts series, two Cecil Murphey books, and Love is a Verb Devotional by Gary Chapman.

In 2018, I published my memoir, *Praying for Murder, Receiving Mercy: From At-Risk to At Peace; My Journey from Fear to Freedom.* From the feedback I've received, I know this book has helped countless women in at-risk relationships, single moms, and the people who love them. Of the paperbacks that have sold, many buyers say they passed their copies on to others who need them. However, I won't know the full impact of God's story in my life until I get to heaven.

I've had articles published in regional, Christian, and secular magazines such as *Country, Guideposts, War Cry, Focus on the Family* and FOTF's *Clubhouse, Just Between Us, Christian Communicator magazines, Sasee, Fate,* and more. My articles have been on websites such as CBN.com, Charismamag.com, ThrivingFamily.com, and ReadersDigest.com.

I am on the blog team for Mentoring Moments for Christian Women. From the 1990s through 2014, I wrote consistently for weekly newspapers. I have enjoyed speaking to women's groups, teenagers, and teachers since 1987, and currently speak throughout the southeastern USA. I belong to Word Weavers International writers' critique group. My website is www.kellystigliano.com.

I married my first husband when I was 18 years old. After five years I became a single mother and later married my current husband, Jerry.

I am a Christian who writes through that worldview. My writing is like my humor - sometimes a bit edgy. I'm not a "big name" nor am I a novice.

As with anything you do, sift through this content and find what works for you.

Now! With that out of the way, let's move forward. Let's enjoy a friendly chat!

CHAPTER ONE

Groundwork for Success

Groundwork is essential to the success of any task. A contractor will tell you the process of preparing the sub-surfaces for the start of a building project is crucial to bear the weight of the structure. Different aspects of the basis for construction include ground investigation, site clearance, and foundation. So groundwork for your writing is to sort out (investigate) what stands in your way, deal with it (site clearance), and solidify the ground for the foundation. So let's get started.

If you are hesitant or unsure or just plain scared to write, let's figure out why. I'm not your counselor, but I can suggest where to start. First, pray to God and ask Him to show you what stands in your way and why. That's the investigation. Possibly someone said something that made you doubt your ability to write.

Let's clear the site. Ask yourself, "When did I first hear the lie?" What lie? You know—the lie that you wouldn't be successful in your life. The lie that you can't write or aren't creative. Did you have a teacher or parent who were overly critical and spoke destruction into your life?

In Proverbs in the Bible, verse 18 talks about the power of our words. It says our tongue can bring life or death. So who spoke death into your life? Maybe you overheard someone talking about you and you internalized their words. Think about it for a minute. Perhaps it was more than one time.

When I was little, I had adults say things to me that cut into my spirit and they didn't even know it. They spoke carelessly to a little kid and didn't weigh the consequences. Yet, it stuck. As I grew up, the enemy, Satan, (I told you I write through a Christian worldview and this is it) took note of that wound and reinforced it whenever he could. I made bad choices throughout my life until I finally recognized them and asked God to forgive me. I gave Him control over every part of my life. That's what it took to prepare the foundation for Him to use me in life—that includes me sharing what is on my heart and in my spirit.

Ask God to help you clear those rocks of doubt away so you can prepare the foundation for the weight of communicating what He has put on your heart.

Can you relate? If you cannot, please take a minute now and read the last chapter of this book for guidance in allowing God to give you solid ground for the work He has for you. Then, after laying the crucial foundation, you can confidently move forward with your mission to convey what you feel called to share.

CHAPTER TWO

Chain Links

Every day we make decisions. Some are life-altering and require much time and attention. Some are made in haste and we live with the consequences. There are no wasted experiences, regardless of the outcome. Each incident is like a chain link.

In the past, as I have found myself looking for a new job in a new town, I've often felt alone and ill-equipped for the positions I've sought or accepted. However, as they say, "hindsight is 20/20." Now, years later, I can see the hand of God in my options and decisions. Each job, big or small;

each volunteer gig, long-term or short-term, has played an important part in who I am today. Each has been a piece in the puzzle of God's work in my life.

For example, in 1994, due to Jerry's job change, we moved to a village of 2,500 people in West Virginia. I found employment opportunities virtually nonexistent. Having been a secretary in previous years, I set out to find an office job.

The village had one streetlight. Our house was on a hill just north of the intersection. The drive into town took less than two minutes. Exiting my car, I paused and looked up. The sky was brilliant blue and without clouds. "This is going to be a good day. Let's go get a job, God!" However, my confidence was soon shaken.

Walking into a large bank, I approached the employee at the customer service desk. "I'd like to complete an application, please."

Without raising her head, she glared over her glasses. "No."

"May I leave my resume for your HR Dept?"

She rolled her eyes and laughed. "We haven't hired here in years. No one leaves their job." She wouldn't even take my resume.

After a few attempts at other businesses, I recognized a trend. Desperate for employment, I even applied to clean hotel rooms. As the rude lady at the bank had said, people didn't leave their posts and I couldn't find work anywhere.

At that time I was irritated at the situation, the people, the town, and ultimately the state. Now I know that it was God. He wasn't against me—He had a better plan for me. You see, a few months later the volunteer Development Director of the Christian school my kids attended was feeling overwhelmed.

While cleaning her kitchen after dinner with her family, she was complaining to God about her over-burdened schedule. As she wiped the countertops, she prayed. "God, I need help."

"Offer Kelly the job," popped into her head. Not knowing if I'd found employment yet or not, she phoned me. We met later that week for coffee and she offered me a job as her assistant. She let me choose my hours and my wage, and paid me herself because she needed help.

As her assistant I learned how to write newspaper articles, ads for billboards, radio spots, brochures, and all their correspondence, as well as manage their database.

Without that opportunity, I wouldn't have been able to get several jobs that followed, as we moved to other states. With the knowledge I garnered through that position, I have been able to serve in several volunteer situations.

Each job and volunteer appointment, as uncomfortable or insignificant as it may have seemed at the time, turned out to be a link in the chain that has led me to where I am today. Each helped me grow personally, professionally, and even spiritually.

Whether you find yourself employed or unemployed at this time, think about what you are learning. Consider your past jobs and decisions, and try to see a pattern. Did your first volunteer post help build your self-confidence and people skills, thus equipping you for job number one? Was there one small added responsibility in that position that cinched job number two? Did job number two provide the experience necessary to get job number three?

If we forget about what we want and concentrate on what God wants for us, we will begin to see His influence in our lives and it will help us make positive decisions for our futures. If we deal with the lies that have held us back/stifled our creativity, we can begin the journey to our God-ordained destiny.

Don't know where to start? Take fifteen minutes a day and write about anything. Don't edit; just write!

Balance

In 1985, I remarried. The following year my husband, Jerry took a position as the principal of a Christian school in Rochester, New York. I worked as a secretary through a temporary agency and settled into a long-term part-time job in the Special Government Contracts department of Eastman Kodak. The building was massive and required much walking. I enjoyed it and loved my coworkers.

Simultaneously, I worked part-time for a commercial equipment auctioneer. His office was in the basement of a bank and I transcribed notes from the recordings he made while conducting inventories at factories in preparation for their auctions. I had no coworkers. The basement office was quiet and laid back, with little movement on my part.

Even with those two jobs, I was restless. I wanted to be at home when my children returned from school each day. Because Jerry was their principal, they went to work with him early in the mornings and came back with him each afternoon. As a single mom I had worked many hours and now I wanted to spend as much time with them as possible.

After I'd worked at Kodak for a few months, Mary Lou, a co-worker, returned from maternity leave. She was sad to come back to work and leave her two small children with a babysitter. She mentioned the relaxed atmosphere in the home of her caregiver. That ignited a plan in my heart.

Having been a working mom since before my marriage to Jerry, I knew what it was to have poor childcare and I knew what parents wanted for their kids.

I researched what it took to run a New York State-licensed daycare at my house. I got certified by the state and joined a home daycare providers' organization where I learned about age-appropriate activities and the business side of the service. I signed up for their food co-op, purchasing food, paper supplies, and diapers for pennies on the dollar. I signed up for the USDA program for meal reimbursement. I bought appropriate infant furniture, books, and toys. I was ready to give my notice at Kodak.

On a normal dreary day, hence the old joke of Rochester being Kodak's darkroom, employees from my team and surrounding departments took me to lunch. They said sweet words of appreciation and gave me gold earrings. I felt genuinely loved. Still, I was eager to start my position as a self-employed home daycare director.

As a new childcare provider, I slowly grew my clientele of families. With a 6:00 AM to 6:00 PM schedule, I was there when my kids left for school and when they returned home. It was exhausting, but I was doing what I wanted. My children were happy and my little charges were well cared for. Consequently, their parents were happy, too.

Amidst days full of planned activities, I found a new appreciation for toddler books. I loved the enjoyment the colorful volumes brought to the kids.

I'd like to write a children's book, I thought. That sparked a new interest. I signed up for a correspondence course to learn to write for children and began to make small payments for the class. The instructor assigned to me was considerate, honest, and helpful. Unfortunately, due to my draining schedule, I was sluggish in sending in the homework. I couldn't balance my time.

When I got a letter announcing my instructor's resignation, I was disappointed. I truly loved her kind guidance. A new one was appointed to me and she changed everything the previous one had said. It felt like starting over again. It was frustrating, but I knew it was my fault for not returning my work according to schedule.

Perhaps due to a clerical glitch, I received the graduation certificate before I completed the course. I felt scammed and put the last two, unfinished assignments in a closet. I doubted everything I'd been told about my abilities.

My insecurities flourished and those old lies of failure flooded in. I didn't try to write. Time marched on and the canvas bag with reams of coursework moved to another state with us and found a place in a new closet in a new home.

Although that may seem like the end of a dream, what I learned throughout the course was invaluable. Bits and pieces of each lesson stuck in my mind, to my writing benefit. My life education was enhanced, as well.

If your goals are God-inspired, no one can steal them. If Satan tries to use those around you to discourage you, don't allow it. If you allow your busy schedule to sidetrack you, knock it off! Focus. Keep writing. Do better than I did. Don't give up!

CHAPTER FOUR

Educate Yourself

Education is valuable. I'm not saying every person who wants to write should pursue a degree in creative writing. Education comes in many forms and people learn in different ways.

My friend Suzanne says her ADD kept her from learning in school. Now, as a grandmother, she says the world is her classroom. She learns from traveling across the globe. She is a natural observer and her style of schooling helps her write comedy.

When I was in junior and senior high schools, I loved English classes; literature and creative writing were my favorites. I loved to write short stories and even presented a book report on a novel that didn't exist. I fabricated a work of fiction and wrote about it within an hour. It yielded a remarkably good grade. Although not a shining moment in my life, I share the story just to drive home my immersion in writing.

Soon after graduation I became a pregnant teen bride, so post-high-school education wasn't part of my life until I divorced and became a single mom of two pre-schoolers. Then I went to business school to learn to support my little trio. One of the things I studied was English and I fell in love with words all over again. Although I liked to write in school, that passion had been shut away throughout my volatile first marriage of five years.

Even now, over three decades later, I continue to seek opportunities to learn. I attend workshops and conferences. I have watched many free webinars. At the end of each, a course or product is offered for sale. I don't buy what they are selling, but I routinely glean great information from the free parts.

There are many websites for authors, as well as social media groups to join. Sign up for emails from respected professionals you feel you'd like to learn from. Jerry Jenkins' website is helpful, as is Marnie Swedberg at Marnie.com.

I have a cache of books ranging from self-promotion to grammar, from quotations to the basics like dictionaries and various thesauruses. I also use my Comparative Study Bible and Bible Commentaries. While some may feel actual books are passé, I appreciate them when our power goes out. I live in hurricane-prone Florida. With the physical editions, I can still research and write. I blow the dust off the volumes, grab a pencil and paper, and keep at it.

Because of the myriad distractions wifi affords, some writers turn it off while writing. No notifications or temptations to check email. Pretending it is 1990 can be refreshing!

When our kids were in high school, our son was supposed to attend a writers' convention with another student and their English teacher, Mrs. Tyler. My son got sick and the other student refused to go alone. The teacher and I went instead.

While chatting with an author who'd been published in Guideposts magazine, I pointed out that I'd never had anything exciting happen in my life to warrant a Guideposts article. Mrs. Tyler snapped her head around to me. "That's what YOU think!"

I didn't get it. Why would she say that? She didn't know me that well. That comment, combined with a few others I'd heard, changed my mind about writing. *Maybe I can do it. Maybe I do have something to say after all.*

Sometimes our lessons come in difficulties. When my family and I lived in a city, I wrote an opinion letter to the editor of the large daily newspaper and it was well received. However, when we lived in a community 240 times smaller, I wrote an opinion letter to the editor of the weekly paper and it created an emotional uproar within the community.

I had discovered a deception in a local business and the complicity of the employees. The reasoning behind the fraudulent reporting was outrageous. I felt my points were valid and well presented, but they were not accepted. Beyond not being accepted, I was verbally attacked. The response from local leadership, as well as the school board that employed my husband, was complex. Looking back, it's what, I, as a Christian, call spiritual abuse. It affected me spiritually, emotionally, and even physically. It took a few months to pull myself together.

When we moved from that place, the school board wouldn't give Jerry his severance pay until I signed a letter they'd written, which said I would not write anything about their town. Apparently, I wrote with authority and that made them nervous. I cannot tell you the sense of power that gave me! We needed the money and I signed it. My confidence grew exponentially through that nightmare.

Similar to what Joseph told his brothers in the Bible, in Genesis 50:20, what was intended to harm me and break my spirit, God used for good—my good and that of others.

Use your trials to fuel your gift. Share your lessons and help others grow.

At a writers' conference I attended years later, one of the speakers was well-known author, Karen O'Conner. I paid a little more to have her critique a portion of a manuscript I was working on at that time. She was honest and compassionate. She asked why I would start with such an ambitious project as a book and suggested I shoot for articles first. I kept that advice in the back of my mind.

After we moved to another state, I received a direct mail piece about a correspondence course offered by Long Ridge Writers Group. The card had a pencil drawing of one of their instructors. It was Karen O'Conner! While I knew I wouldn't get her for my teacher, I signed up and took the course called Breaking into Print. It focused on getting published in magazines. I plugged along and did well. Nearly all of my assignments eventually found homes in paying markets. Many became workshops I'd present later. Long Ridge is now called IFW, Institute for Writers.

Recognize the green lights. Stay teachable and don't be afraid to invest in improving your gift. You don't have to spend loads of money. Take a free class online, join a writers' group, and read books on your craft. Even if your circumstances change, your goals probably will not. Rise to the challenge and don't give up.

Do you think you have nothing worthwhile to say? Rethink your experiences. When I started writing about my life and the lessons learned, I found publishing success.

People can benefit from the things you've been through in your life, be they achievements or mistakes.

Maybe you're depriving others of a blessing or opportunity for growth. Hold nothing back!

CHAPTER FIVE

Your Voice

It feels safer to have someone read your writing when they don't know it's you. You can essentially hide when your name isn't connected with your words. That's why cyberbullying is rampant. But that's not you. You want to express what is burning in your soul. You want to share your story, even if it's exclusively for your family. If you're writing a memoir, you have experiences to recount and lessons to impart. Your descendants deserve to know—it's their family history.

Whether fiction or nonfiction, sharing your manuscript is scary. A supportive writers' group should be your safe place; a place to show your writings without fear of ridicule. That is a great place to find your voice – your unique style of writing.

Perhaps you woke up from a dream or had a revelation during the day and realized it would make a great novel. There's that burning again. You cannot rest until you get it onto paper or into your computer. Your fingers float over the keyboard like a musician playing a concerto. It's your narrative and you have to declare it.

There are many things we can learn from studying other authors. We can learn how they describe people, places, or events. We can analyze their use of dialogue and dialect. Readers make good writers, true. However, when you write, don't try to emulate your favorite novelist. You are one-of-a-kind and the more you practice, the more you will develop a distinctive tone to your prose.

When I wrote newspaper pieces for the Christian school in West Virginia, I didn't have a byline because it was one of my duties for the office of development. My boss and I took turns submitting articles to the local weekly paper. We wrote about what the students were doing and their community involvement, highlighted students and teachers, and covered sporting events.

One chilly morning after attending a meeting at the school, I stood outside chatting with the parents. We each pulled our jackets closed and pushed our hands deep into our pockets. Our breath momentarily hung in the air as we spoke. Some sipped warm coffee. One of the moms approached me. She smiled sweetly. "I liked your article this week."

I beamed. "Thank you!" I silently wondered how she knew it was mine because my name wasn't on it.

"I knew it was yours because I recognized your style."

I was surprised. My style? I didn't realize I had a style!

I thanked her again, wished her well, and headed back to my car with a little hop. Climbing in, I cranked up the heater. I couldn't stop smiling.

I had diligently done my best to cover activities, shining the spotlight on others. Through that process, my unique voice emerged.

Years later when I wrote for the weekly paper in northeastern Florida, people asked my boss for me to cover their events. They appreciated the casual, friendly, "homey" tone to my writing.

If you ghostwrite something, the "author" can expect your original voice to come through. I did that one time. I encouraged my sister-in-law to share her angel experience with one of Chicken Soup for the Soul's angel editions. I took the notes she had for a presentation she gave at her church. She had shared the event at family Christmas so I rounded it out with dialogue from the conversation she'd mentioned. The story was accepted for publication. Because Chicken Soup doesn't do "as told to" stories, my name wasn't on the piece. Still, my style bled through.

Be yourself. Write in your own voice. It is exclusive to you — it's your style.

The Right Time

There are seasons in our lives that ordain our paths. Perhaps when your kids are little you'll have less time to write. Maybe you can squeeze in a half hour of writing on your lunch break at work each day. You will find out what time of day works best for you.

I'm a morning person. It seems if I don't get things done by 10:00 AM, my day is shot. For me, time flies by after that golden hour. That doesn't mean I'm always productive, but it is my goal.

Some people find their best writing time is at night. Even if you only have fifteen minutes, simply write. Don't spend time editing at first. Just get your thoughts out.

When I was a child, I was described as "hyper" and I could sense the tension from my authority figures. Years later I began to hear about "ADD" and "ADHD." I could somewhat identify and pondered how my life might have been different if adults had considered my misbehavior a medical concern instead of a social annoyance. However, I refuse to cry over spilt milk. Moving forward, I strive for some productivity each day. That also means managing my emotions.

I used to struggle with rejection letters from magazine editors. When I'd receive one, I'd put the article away for a long time while I "licked my wounds" like an injured animal. I can't tell you the exact time that stopped, but it eventually did. It stung less and less. Occasionally a kind editor would take a few seconds to note his or her opinion on my story. That was dearly appreciated.

When God is telling you to write something, you must—you must obey or you'll feel miserable.

The first big thing I wrote was what I'd hoped would be a book. It would be a "how-to" book for newly-single mothers. Before I received Karen O'Connor's critique, I had submitted portions of the manuscript to editors and agents. I couldn't take rejection then and every time I'd get a negative response, the manuscript sat for months. I never finished it.

Years later at a mission conference in Florida, I saw a book like the one I was supposed to write. Even the title was nearly the same. My heart broke.

I realized that if God wants something done, He'll find someone to do it. It was written in spite of me.

There are many books on every subject. I certainly could have proceeded with my manuscript, but my broken heart shut down my ambition. No, obviously my ambition was gone long before then or I would have carried on with that initial book idea.

I'm sitting here confessing to you, compassionate reader, that I have no good excuse for walking away from that manuscript. I should have taken the book at that mission conference as a sign to complete my version! It would've had my opinions, my experiences, my VOICE.

Thankfully, portions of my long-forgotten manuscript went into my memoir later.

Feel called to write? Get at it! If God wants it done, it'll get done. No rejection or negativity is worth years of procrastination and disobedience. Nothing feels as good as obeying God.

As writers we must develop thick skin and broad shoulders to push through the rejections. That takes prayer.

Tick-tock. Tick-tock. Your dreams may not change, but the world around you will. Don't give up!

CHAPTER SEVEN

Finding Your Place

When we lived in a small town in North Carolina, I started writing for a children and family newspaper that reported on the positive things kids did. The paper came out twice a month.

Although I covered more sports than I cared to, I loved it. Taking photographs to accompany each article kept it interesting. The families were always excited to see their children in the paper.

We moved to Florida and I wrote for our county's weekly newspaper. I started with the religion section and branched out to all things fluff. "Happy crap," I called it. I enjoyed it because I met many interesting people, was afforded admission to fun events, and my ego liked being asked for personally when the paper was involved.

I wrote features about new stores, churches, pastors, ministries, etc. I found that my forte was making people look good and I loved "tooting their horns."

One day my role was clarified. I learned that I was a writer working for a newspaper for income, not a reporter who wrote magazine articles on the side.

While sitting in a restaurant early one morning, interviewing a couple about a sports tournament fundraiser they were planning, there was an accident in the parking lot. A man working on a light was shocked and fell to the ground. He didn't move. Someone ran to me and told me to go take pictures; she said I could "scoop" the story.

I was mortified. I did not run out to take his picture. "Scooping" others wasn't important to me at that point. I prayed for him. He lived, by the way.

If you find yourself in the middle of a job or assignment and realize it's not your cup of tea, don't worry. Like the links in a chain mentioned in chapter two, there are elements of your experience that will benefit you later.

Additionally, you don't have to pigeonhole yourself into one genre. When Jerry and I discovered Frank Peretti's novels, we delved into his mesmerizing version of Christians living in the world of supernatural beings. Then I learned he had originally written adventure stories for children. It was when we read his fabulous memoir called *The Wounded Spirit* that I fully appreciated his extensive writing talents.

We are flexible, complex individuals with much to say. Don't try to be something you're not. Stay true to yourself. Spread your wings. Try different kinds of writing and you'll find your niche or your range. Just write!

CHAPTER EIGHT

Where Do I Submit?

There are wonderful resources for finding where to submit your writing. I purchase the Christian Writers Market Guide every other year.

Don't worry if your Guide is not the current year. Magazines and websites go out of business often. You will at least see the basic information that will help with your online research. And do always explore each publication online first because contact details change continually.

On the Institute for Writers website you can find resources including courses, blogs for writers, and books on writing.

I hesitate to share websites or emails because things change so quickly. There are many websites that list writers' markets. Allfreelancewriting.com is a good resource.

Opportunities for publication come in my email. Sally Clark shares information regularly. Contact her at sally@sallyclark.info to sign up for her helpful emails. Another great one is Hope Clark. Go to fundsforwriters.com, and click on the "Newsletter" tab to sign up for her newsletters which are full of helpful data including grants available for writers. If you're eager to be considered for Chicken Soup for the Soul editions, go to their website, click the "Submit Your Story" tab at the bottom of the page and you will see what books they are planning and the guidelines and deadlines for each.

To combat the temptation to sulk after receiving a rejection, I keep a list of which publications I will target next. Some accept simultaneous submissions; some do not. Your research will clarify that.

As soon as I receive a "thanks, but no thanks" response, I read the piece again, improve it as I can, (this is where being part of good writers' critique group helps), and shoot it out to the next magazine on the list. I keep a chart of what article I sent to whom, when it was sent, when it was accepted or rejected, and if applicable, when payment was received and when it was published. This helps me not duplicate my efforts and helps me see which magazines to return to with new articles.

A word about payments. Unfortunately, more and more e-zines, magazines, and journals are "paying" with a link to your website in your bio, and complimentary copies.

Exposure is not to be downplayed. When you are first starting and need to build your list of credits for that all-important platform, this is fine. However, some adamantly proclaim that writers should never write for free; that it hurts everyone. I see both sides of the argument. I also see that assembling a list of reputable credits is essential to be considered for print – and payment – by bigger publications. One has to decide where to draw the line on freebies. It's a conundrum.

Can the average writer make money as an article/story writer? Yes, but I've found that, for me, it's never been much money. I've written for newspapers and magazines, mostly. While secular magazines pay, I'm sorry to say Christian magazines don't pay much, if at all. The ones I've found success with, the Assembly of God magazines, Salvation Army's War Cry, and Focus on the Family, pay decently.

Popular secular magazines pay much better. I believe that once you've gotten your first article printed in one of them, they'll welcome you back. Amber Petty offers a course on writing wherein she has links to secular publications that pay. Check her out at AmberPetty.com.

The compilation books I've contributed to have paid between $10 and $250, plus books. I have heard that some pay more.

Sometimes little-known authors will have people pay them to be part of their anthologies. If you encounter that, RUN AWAY! While some may suggest it's alright to pay if you feel it's beneficial to be part of the author's work, I'm still calling shenanigans on that practice. In my opinion, you should never pay to be part of a publication that will yield income for someone else. Remember the "Who's Who in (insert organization's name here)" books? You give them money and you can have an edition with your name in it. No. Just, no.

Being part of a "big-name" author's compilation should pay something, even if it's only $10.

So can you support yourself by writing for magazines? I've not found that to be true, but that's me. I have read articles from authors who solely support themselves that way. Maybe I'm not talented enough or don't work hard enough. Maybe I lack the right connections. But you are you. Don't take my lack of stardom as your own. We each have our own path.

I have come to realize that there are many more people making money *from* writers than *as* writers. Use your God-given discernment before paying for anything writing-related. Be judicial when selecting writers' conferences and contests that charge an entry fee. Certainly do consider them, just be selective.

Very early on I had a publishing house contact me about producing a manuscript I had presented at a writers' conference. Their representative contacted me so quickly, I was suspicious. Every other house represented at the event had rejected me. While talking to the man on the phone, I agreed to receive their contract in the mail and read it over. It came via Priority Mail Express. Frankly, that was another red flag. Why was this guy in such a hurry?

I read the paperwork and realized it was what we called a vanity publishing company. I was to pay them a large sum of money; they'd publish my manuscript and, in time, give me a small percentage of sales. They would allow one round of edits. They didn't offer marketing. They only promised a handful of distributors.

As soon as I received their package, the representative called me again. I told him I'd have to discuss it with my husband. He said, no. He said I'd have to commit over the phone at that moment, sign the paperwork immediately, and take it to the post office. Having escaped a marriage comprised of gaslighting, manipulations, coercion, and straight-up brainwashing, I swallowed the ugly words I wanted to blast him with and replied with a curt, but polite, "no, thank you" and hung up the phone.

I later read dozens of bad reviews from desperate writers who had unfortunately fallen for that company's tactics.

There are many publishing promises out there. They are not all dishonest. Please pray about each choice, read all the reviews, check with the Better Business Bureau, talk to other writers, and proceed cautiously. JustPublishingAdvice.com is a good resource for many things including how to spot a scam.

If you feel like you've made a poor choice and have been taken advantage of, take a deep breath and move on. We've all made expensive mistakes. I mean it. No matter what someone tells you, we all have.

Still, don't be discouraged. Keep writing. You write for yourself first; as an act of obedience to that God-given call. If you put it all in God's hands, you'll land where you're supposed to. That may be small beans like me or top of the heap like Debbie Macomber or Stephen King, or somewhere in between. Just do your best, obey God, and write what you're supposed to write.

Don't be mercenary or overly competitive. Remember we're all writers trying to do our best. There are plenty of writing outlets out there for everyone. Always cheer others on to be their best, too. Be an encourager!

CHAPTER NINE

Choose the Voice You Are Listening To

In 1998, after I'd had a few articles published in magazines, I was in a bookstore with my daughter who was in college. She perused anthologies; collections of stories about one particular topic or focus. There were mom anthologies and pet anthologies. There were compilation books containing humorous stories about school days and family dynamics.

"Mom, you should try to get into one of these books. This is the kind of stuff you write. You could do it."

Why do the voices of my children speak louder than other voices in my life? I don't know, but I took her advice and started submitting to compilation books. Success slowly followed.

Then my daughter said I should write a blog.

"Many books have come from collections of blog posts, Mom."

Although I haven't written my own, for a while I maintained the religion blog for the weekly newspaper I worked for. It was fun and I had intriguing interactions with readers. Still, to write my own was a different story.

"I don't think I have anything exciting to say on an ongoing basis. I have no children at home. I'm not a foodie; unless you consider Hebrew National fat-free hot dogs baked in crescent rolls a delicacy. I'm not in the middle of an interesting social experiment." I talked myself out of it.

Decades earlier, a series of poor choices led me to the wedding altar as a pregnant teenager. Within the first month I realized I was married to a misogynist and the worst was yet to come.

Being hit in the head, choked, and told I was worthless took a toll. By the time I grabbed my two babies and escaped from my marriage of disparage, I had no self-esteem left. I believed I could do nothing right.

As a single mother, I attended business school. Armed with a secretarial science certificate, I was ready to interview for jobs. It was 1983.

I sat in a posh office. Three well-dressed people looked over my resume. Their haircuts were fresh and stylish.

I felt ugly in my cheap polyester suit; my stringy hair pulled into a bun.

"Did you write your own resume?"

I didn't understand the simple question because I'd never heard of companies that do that for you.

"Yes?" I replied with trepidation.

"Well, you're a good writer."

Was he trying to trick me? It was just my resume. I honestly didn't get it and trusted no one.

"Thank you," I whispered and looked at the floor.

"It's well-written and concise."

I shrugged my shoulders. "Really? Thank you."

"Well, we're interviewing through next week and will get back to you."

I shook their hands and thanked them for the third time.

Walking to my car, my stomach twisted. I was suspicious. Was he making fun of me? I enjoyed writing in junior and senior high school. I loved the English portion of my business school education. *Maybe he meant it*, I thought. I tucked his words into my heart.

I didn't get the job. It probably went to someone more polished and confident than me.

Jump forward to 2018. I published my memoir and entered it into a few Christian self-published book contests. I entered it into a secular one, too. The Annual Writer's Digest contests are a pretty big deal.

They all required a book or two, plus an entry fee. I knew they all received my entries because my checks were cashed.

Picture the pages of the calendar flying away like in a cartoon.

One of the Christian contests emailed a list of winners and the entire category of memoir was eliminated, without explanation.

My mind flashed back to my senior year in high school. My Home Economics classmates elected me to the position of president of the FHA. Future Homemakers of America was a thing in those days. The Home Ec teacher was the faculty sponsor. That was the only year the school didn't have FHA. She would rather eliminate the program for that single year than have me be the president. I understood why. I was horrible to her—from mocking her wig with my own David Bowie-style wig to putting chocolate laxatives in her chocolate chip cookies. Believe me, I understood!

This unspoken dismissal of my memoir, however, I did not. Was it because of the "raw" nature of my story; of my life before I met God? Were memoirs supposed to be about roses and sunshine?

When asked why the category was eliminated, she said there weren't enough entries so it was absorbed into another group. Wow. Just, wow.

"Please don't throw my books away. People could benefit from them."

She said she'd donate them to a charity.

The other Christian contests didn't respond either. For competitions based on communication skills, I was surprised.

On the other hand, the big secular contest, Writer's Digest did communicate. They sent a complete awards breakdown with the judging points ranging from one to five, and how I scored on each. I was thrilled to see that my memoir did very well. The email included a long commentary from the judge. Her words were kind and encouraging. Her comments proved that she'd read the entire paperback. The one question she had was answered in the book's introduction. However, without spiritual eyes to see, it was missed.

I chose to listen to her written words as opposed to the unspoken shouts from the others. Two very different responses from those in authority over me.

In the past, their responses, or lack of them, would have put a chink in my armor. Instead, I groused to Jerry about how, although I love the Lord, sometimes I don't love His people. Rant over, I moved on. I didn't waste time on negativity or hurt feelings. Our days are precious and it's not worth it.

I chose to remember the hundreds of people who reported having been helped by my "too raw" book. Real people aren't always good and real life is usually messy.

Did I write my book to win the approval of judges, other writers, or writing groups? No. I had to put myself back on the rails again. I reminded myself that I wrote as an act of obedience to God. Simple, but not easy. Brave, but not without fear.

Consider the opinions in your life and choose which voices to listen to. Then, give writing a try. Submit your best for publication and don't fret about the outcome. If you get a rejection slip, staple it to your copy of the article, and put it into a folder. Make email folders for rejected and accepted articles that come electronically.

After that, shoot a copy and query letter out to the next periodical on your list. Hopefully, you'll receive a line or two of encouragement or suggestion for improvements from a kind-hearted editor. Take the advice and continue to learn, grow, and develop your talent. In time you will be tucking the printed magazine article into that same folder.

Likewise, if you are published and receive a bad review, don't curl up and hibernate like I used to. Consider the reviewer's points and discern if they are valid. If so, purpose to improve on those issues with the help of your writers' critique group. If the review is simply mean-spirited drivel, lift your chin, straighten your back, and carry on. You have no time for the jealous, malevolent barbarians who anonymously attack others. You are far too busy for that. You have a calling to write. Simple, but not easy. Brave, but not without fear.

Failure is another way to grow. Thomas Edison, the inventor of many things, said, "I have not failed, I've just found ten thousand ways that won't work."

CHAPTER TEN

My Story

After I escaped from my violent husband, and my two children and I were on our own, I encountered a freedom I'd never known. It was the early 1980s.

As I tried to heal inside and out, my self-reliance grew. My partying increased and my personal life went off the rails. Finally, on the verge of self-destruction, I noticed God waiting for me. I reached out and gave Jesus control of my out-of-control life. That's when true healing began.

I stopped partying and had most evenings free. After I'd put the children to bed, I wrote poems to God. Similar to the Psalms in the Bible, most started out complaining about my circumstances and ended up praising God and thanking Jesus.

With the help of God, church, and friends, my emotional healing progressed and my spiritual life began to flourish.

After Jerry and I married in 1985 and our lives settled down into a delightful routine of a normal, healthy family, my gratitude exploded.

Remembering how far I'd come— wincing whenever a hand was raised in front of me; constantly saying, "I'm sorry" — I began to write about my experiences. It was writing just for me.

I didn't think I was writing a "memoir" per se. It was therapeutic to get out what I had hidden inside for so long. For ten years I wrote and wrote and wrote. It was like vomiting words onto paper.

Eventually, it became clear to me that others might be helped by hearing my story. God spoke into my heart, directing me to share my journey. (Read more about that in **Chapter Thirteen: Writing a Memoir**.) It would be not only for women who had made bad choices, but also for single mothers. Further, I realized that because of the outcome of my life, it could bring hope to the people who loved, worried about, and prayed for single moms, as well as those in at-risk relationships.

"Ok, God. I hear You. I'll do it." My prayer was one of faith and fear, but I knew I had to obey. By then I had learned that nothing feels as good as obedience to God and He would have my back.

I began to edit, cut, and revise my writing. In time I joined Word Weavers writer's critique group and they did the same. Month after month, year after year, I brought excerpts from my manuscript to the group. We discussed how to deal with the cussing in the dialogue. They helped with grammar and points of view.

I vacillated between making it fiction and non-fiction. Did I ever want to be able to show my face at a family reunion again? Fiction would be safe. Non-fiction would be more helpful to those in similar situations. I prayed a lot, revised a lot, and decided on nonfiction. Finally one of the leaders in my writers' group, who had previously worked as a book editor said, "Kelly, you need to just get this published and stop bringing it for editing every month. You're ready."

Her words sent fear from my head to my toes. It's all fun and games until you have to reveal your "baby" to the world! What if they said my "baby" was ugly? What if people rejected me? What if my writing wasn't good enough? Those old lies flooded back in! No one ever said obedience comes without fear.

I attended Christian writers' conferences and presented portions of my story to editors and agents. I was told that Christian publishing houses wouldn't touch my story because it was too "raw." I was told they won't even allow characters in fiction novels to smoke or use rum in a tiramisu recipe! Certainly, my account of leaving an abusive relationship and going from victim to heathen to victor would never be accepted.

I queried secular publishing houses and agents and learned that they weren't interested in hearing about God in their books. Evidently, they felt there was no money in books about redemption.

For years I shunned the notion of self-publishing. The term "vanity publishing" was hot then and I didn't want to be associated with it.

"If it's good enough to publish, someone will do it," I said. What had been fear morphed into pride. More years ticked by.

Then it happened. Within two years, several people from my past died. Some were friends who, although renamed, were part of my testimony. If I had published my book, perhaps they would have read it. They would have learned how God brought me from fear to faith. Did my disobedience send them to hell? God alone can judge the heart.

I had to move forward. In March of 2018, I hired a skilled editor and she found several errors.

That July I got an email from Focus on the Family ministry. Seven years earlier, they received a recording of me presenting my testimony at a church in Florida, which had been taped three years prior. So by the time they contacted me, the recording was ten years old. They said they were going to play it on their radio program in two parts in October.

I felt an urgency to get the book completed before then. I hired a cover designer. I rushed and started making expensive mistakes. That is explained further in **Chapter Twelve: My Writing and Publishing Mistakes**.

I knew I had to get my story out there and I should publish it myself. I researched hybrid publishers and self-publishing companies. I finally decided to publish independently with IngramSpark. I liked their international distribution outlets.

One last round of content editing was necessary. This one would be the one that threw open the doors to the secrets I'd held captive on the pages of my memoir.

I chose the former writers' group member who had told me to get my manuscript out there. I had never brought the "raw" parts to be critiqued, but I trusted her opinion. She is a leader in her denominational community and I knew she'd give me the hard-line view of many potential readers. She agreed to be a beta reader for me and give me her honest thoughts on it.

My friend took my story with her on vacation. She later returned it with her comments. She said she had nearly walked away from it because it felt like she was reading pornography. While her comments hurt, I knew I needed them. They were exactly why I'd chosen her to proofread it.

I thanked her and set out to eliminate everything she'd mentioned. I saved those deleted sections into a separate file. Maybe someday God will direct me to use them somewhere. I don't know.

Another friend offered to give it a "once over" and I quickly agreed. She is an English professor and I value her expertise. She found a couple of remaining things that would offend the sensitive reader and I made those changes, as well.

I moved forward to publish my memoir and it was available a couple of weeks after the Focus on the Family broadcast. They wouldn't recommend it or add it to their online bookstore, but would provide my website, which linked to that book and all the anthologies to which I'd contributed. I was grateful.

After the release date, many friends contacted me. Most were gracious and even sympathetic. However, two women said they would never find themselves in the position of abused spouse. "I'd never put up with that. I'm way too strong!" I replied directly to them, calling them on their pride. Referring them back to the book, I noted that someone who was not strong would still in that position, or dead.

Between the book and the international radio broadcast, people from across the globe got in touch with me. Their comments were powerful and kind. Strangers and friends shared their trauma from previous and current relationships. My heart broke. Most had prayer requests.

I prayed, "Lord, this is a tiny glimpse into what You hear every day. I can't shoulder the burden."

He instructed me to make a prayer chart on a whiteboard. I wrote the prayer requests, who gave them to me, and from where they came. They became part of my daily prayers.

I drew closer to God. I delved deeper into the Bible, prayed more, and sought the strength that comes only from Him. It made me concentrate on His voice even more. Indeed, you never know how much you need God until He's all you have. I couldn't reach those people, but He could. It was a privilege to bring their names and needs to Him.

So it took twenty years to complete my book. Ten years to write, which was cathartic. Then ten more years to improve it and hide behind edits and rewrites. Twenty years. Please don't procrastinate.

When I finally got my book published, I felt so relieved. It was like an elephant stepped off my chest. I never realized how oppressive disobedience is.

Please don't hesitate to obey God because, as I said, nothing feels as good and freeing as obedience to God!

CHAPTER ELEVEN

Your Support System

It's safe to write and never have anyone read it. There will be a day, however, when you will share your work. You need to decide what that looks like for you. Even if you intend to self-publish, you will need your work professionally edited first. The place to start is with a helpful writers' group.

A writers' critique group is priceless. You could start by joining writers groups on social media and locate one from there. However, you have to find the right one. If you write fiction, it might behoove you to join one specifically for that genre. If you're a Christian, perhaps you'd like to join a Christian writers' group. Please know, however, that not all groups are for everyone. Fortunately, I found a good one on my second try.

The first one was comprised of Christians. That was a match. It was within a half hour from my house and that was good since they met at night. However, they were all men who wrote science fiction. They were caring and thoughtful in their critiques, but it didn't suit me.

Through that group, I learned of a Christian writers' group called Word Weavers International. The one closest to me met in St. Augustine, FL. I lived in a town slightly south of Jacksonville, about an hour away. They met once a month on Saturday mornings. It was comprised of men and women who wrote all genres. The key for me was the variety of people and degree of knowledge within the group. Some were unpublished writers like me. Some were already published. Some were still in school. Some were college professors. I needed that variety. I needed the younger ones to say if they fully understood what I wrote, and the more practiced ones to give me technical and content guidance. To me, it was worth my once-a-month drive to meet.

More people from my area began to attend so they started Word Weavers in Jacksonville. It was nearly as far as St. Augustine because Jacksonville is geographically the largest city in America. After attending for a short time, thankfully someone started a chapter in my county. Again, I was grateful that a college professor attended.

Several people from my Word Weavers groups also attended other writers' critique organizations, both in-person and online. Through their tales, I learned that not all are good. If the people aren't kind in their critiques, patient with explaining the rules, and diligent to ensure everyone follows protocol, it can do more harm than good.

It takes time to be kind. We should never be in too big of a hurry to use all the words necessary to gently guide someone on their path to success—whatever that may be. I have failed in this and regret it to this day.

The biggest thing to take away from this is, if you attend a writers' critique group and don't feel good about it, don't join. You needn't explain your decision to anyone. "I don't feel it's a good fit for me," should be enough. Their response will speak volumes. If they are hostile toward you, you will know you've made the right decision. If they are kind and understanding, perhaps you will recommend them to other writers looking for support.

Attend another and another until you find one that makes you comfortable. When I say "comfortable," I don't mean a group that fawns over your writing and tells you it's perfect. Your grandmother will do that for you. You need honest critique, helpful guidance, and kind responses. You need a group that respects your time and doesn't run over time month after month. You need one that holds the rules and boundaries firm for everyone.

You, in turn, need to understand and respect the rules. Only then can it be a mutually beneficial relationship. Only then will you grow in your craft and progress on your path to publication.

The Word Weavers groups I've belonged to haven't been perfect, but the people have been gentle with their evaluations and guidance. Nearly everything I've taken for review has found publication and that's what it's all about.

There is much to say about supporting yourself. Ignore the lying voice that tells you that you can't write. Ignore the chant that cries that you have nothing important to say.

Through the years, that has been difficult for me. Some call it "positive self-talk," some call it "affirmations," and some call it "personal empowerment." I call it ignoring the voice of the enemy of my soul and "taking every thought captive," as mentioned in 2 Corinthians in the Bible. But, it's easier said than done sometimes.

While on vacation one year, I was at a gift shop in Mt. Airy, North Carolina, and saw wall decals. One, in particular, caught my eye. I bought it and put it up when I repainted my home office. It says, "WISH IT . . . DREAM IT . . . DO IT." At first I was embarrassed to have it on my wall, but I got over it.

A few years later I saw a nine-inch rectangular plaque on the sale rack at a card shop. It said "dreams do come true" and could hold a little square photo. Something told me to buy it. I put it in my file cabinet drawer and thought maybe someday I would have a book published and then – and only then – would I put it on my wall.

When I published my memoir, I had the pleasure of bringing ten donated copies to a local shelter for women in at-risk circumstances. Someone took a photo of me in the lobby holding the stack of books. Yep, you guessed it.

That little plaque with that photo in it now hangs under my wall decal.

When I feel discouraged, I read the words, look at the photo, and remember that God is in the driver's seat of this mission, not me. He never lets me down. He is the most supportive entity in my life. All glory goes to Him for my successes.

CHAPTER TWELVE

My Writing and Publishing Mistakes

For the past couple of years, I've jokingly said, "I should write a book on what NOT to do when self-publishing!" Well here is a chapter dedicated to my mistakes, and expensive mistakes they were. Still, my loving husband reminded me that even though I wasted a good bit of money learning through trial and error, it was still less money than hybrid publishers charged to do it for me.

Hybrid publishers sell packages to writers. They offer services from editing and publishing to a full complement of everything you will need. It sounds like a dream come true. I'm sure it's better than a gourmet breakfast in bed; better than new tires on your vehicle; a stress-free stroll through airport security; a sleeping baby on a cool rainy day, a yummy mug of hot chocolate with mini marshmallows in front of a fire with Christmas music playing. You get the picture. If you can afford it, that's great. However, it isn't in our budget, but "trial and error" is. I learned to wash my own windows without streaks and I can learn to publish my own books, thank you very much.

First, a couple of things I learned while writing the content of *Praying for Murder, Receiving Mercy.* Music was always a big part of my life. Throughout my youth both before and after meeting Jesus, I always had a soundtrack playing in my mind.

In many of the chapters of my memoir manuscript, I had the title, artist, and a line or two of lyrics that punctuated the scene. I learned that you cannot even have one line of a song without paying for it. Nope, not one line.

I researched the production companies of the songs I whittled it down to. I asked them how much it would cost to write a line or two. Most responded. A couple asked to see the manuscript first. Fair enough. One gave me a price of a few hundred dollars. Considering my book was already way too long, it was the impetus I needed to cut the lines out. I simply mentioned the name of the song and artist and said how it was fitting to the situation. That worked well.

For instance in chapter thirty, "How Low Can I Go," I wrote, "My second job was getting complicated. I needed the money, but was it worth the risk? The Rush song 'Freewill' raged in my head. Clearly I needed to make a choice."

Also, from chapter thirty-three, "New People, Ageless God," I wrote, "Songs of freedom resonated throughout my being. 'Trust and Obey' was a necessary reminder when I felt discouraged. 'Love Lifted Me' kept the realization of my rebirth fresh in my mind."

The next thing to consider was this: would I end up in court for using real people in my personal real story about my actual real life? I researched this for days. I spoke with authors and read from authors, agents, and lawyers. One of the most helpful articles came from Helen Sedwick's author page. I hesitate to repeat what I discovered because things change and I wouldn't want to give you bad intel. As always, research for yourself.

For me, I changed the names to respect the innocent and protect the guilty. I had a salty quip in the book that said, "If you recognize yourself in this book and don't like the depiction, maybe you should have been a nicer person" or something like that. Yeah, I took it out. Why poke the bear, right?

Book quotes are allowed, within reason. Remember to always credit from where or whom you quote. Research that, too.

Although my Word Weavers group helped critique my manuscript chapter by chapter—for literally years—I knew I still needed a professional editor.

Mistake number one, I did not research editors. There are qualified editors right under my nose. There are some in Word Weavers International. There are many in the several writers' groups I belong to on social media. I don't know why, but that never occurred to me. I've listed a few recommended by Word Weavers at the end of this chapter.

I went to Fiverr.com because I like the concept. Fiverr.com is "a whole world of freelance talent at your fingertips." Professionals from across the globe share their skills for a good price.

The editor I employed caught some important things to change. She missed a lot, too though. For her time and talents, I paid $1,050. It was a fair price for 2018 for a manuscript as long as mine—just over 100,000 words. Still, I had to go over the manuscript a few more times and caught more errors. Honestly, the book still has mistakes. I take comfort when I see flaws in books written by "big-name" authors. It happens. This book will probably not be perfect either.

Then I got the email from Focus on the Family, referred to earlier. They planned to play my testimony in October on their radio broadcast. They would direct listeners to my website and link it from their webpage.

I felt an urgency to get the book completed. That's when the real mistakes started happening. It is true that "haste makes waste."

I needed someone to design my cover. Returning to Fiverr, I chose (username) "vikncharlie" from the UK. They are proficient and quick. I love my book cover! The initial work was very reasonably priced. The subsequent format changes for eBooks and promotional items were affordable, as well.

I purchased an ISBN number from Bowker online. I bought one for the paperback version for $125. I realized I needed a separate one for the eBook version and purchased another one for $125. Silly choice because they offered ten ISBNs for $295!

I wanted postcard-sized cards with my book cover on them for promotional purposes. After I bought some from VistaPrint for a decent price, I realized they didn't have my website or the Apple Butter Publications logo and name on the back. Had to order more. Cha-ching! The cash register in my head was sounding the alarm.

Things were moving smoothly and I thought time was on my side. Then it happened. I needed the manuscript formatted for IngramSpark, which is a bit tricky for someone who has never done it. That would be me. I decided instead of taking the time to learn, I'd have someone from Fiverr do it.

I chose a woman from America. She wasn't the most experienced on the site. She wasn't the cheapest, but I liked the idea of giving the job to a woman. Yes, sadly I was profiling. I'm not proud of that. But I was reprimanded for my bias when she absolutely couldn't do what was necessary. I'd wasted valuable time and $105.

I returned to the site and chose a man with many more transactions. He did the job quickly and well. I uploaded the manuscript to IngramSpark for both the book and eBook. I uploaded the covers, too. Then I waited to see if it was accepted. It was and although I was in a hurry, I ordered one book to proof before ordering more.

I paid for one book and shipping. Consequently, I paid $25 for one book; another expensive move. However, when I received the book, I was elated that I'd made that choice.

You would have thought I'd never looked at a book. I cringe as I type this. First, let me explain. Maybe it'll hurt less that way. I had been submitting articles and stories for nearly twenty years by this time. Every submission had to be double-spaced. Well, you guessed it. The book came back DOUBLE SPACED! It was huge! I cried as my face burned with humiliation.

Again, sweet Jerry assured me it was ok. So I went back to the computer to try to reformat the entire thing. That changed the lines, pages, everything.

I sent it back to the formatter and he reformatted it again, for a price. Once more, I ordered one book just to check. Meanwhile, the weeks were flying by and my stomach acids splashed up into my throat.

I was disappointed when the proof came back with errors. The formatter didn't double-check before sending it back to me. Wouldn't it be handy if I could stop the story there? But we all know it wasn't ultimately his fault—it was mine. It was my job to double and triple-check his work before uploading it to IngramSpark. Oh, by the way, every upload was $25 more. Cha-ching!

One more round of formatting, me closely checking his work, and another upload later, I was confident enough to order one hundred copies.

I got the cases of books and was so nervous. Jerry and I opened one box. I slowly lifted a book out. I held the cover; stroked the cover; admired the cover; turned the cover over. So far so good. I opened the book. It is written in two parts with photographs (black and white because color is too expensive) in the center. It . . . just . . . didn't . . . look . . . right.

I grabbed a book from my bookshelf. It was written by fellow Word Weaver, Jenifer Jennings. Her books are self-published and look so pretty. What was the difference? Mine was ugly. It looked like a term paper.

Jenifer puts the chapter titles in lovely little flourishes. They're in a pretty font, too. My chapters started at the top of the page like a high school English assignment.

And I had one hundred of them.

I returned to my computer to reformat again. I dropped each chapter title down and added the little picture of apple butter in a jar that the cover designer had put on the front cover. I had chosen Apple Butter Publications as my publishing company name because apple butter is significant in my story. I asked the folks who designed my cover to put it on the back of my book, too. That was an additional fee, albeit small.

After making that change, I sent it to the document formatter again. We went back and forth a couple of times because every time he made a change, it threw something else off. It was tedious, but I was determined there would be no more formatting errors.

I uploaded the updated manuscript, covers for the book and eBook, and (cha-ching!) some more uploading fees later, it was ready. Because I felt I was out of time, I ordered one with expedited shipping, costing $37.

After seeing that one, I was happy and ordered one hundred more for book signings.

So I had one hundred copies that had formatting errors that I didn't want to sell at speaking engagements or signings. I decided to offer them at a discount for donations to women's shelters, etc. The cost of printing and shipping was covered and one hundred women were blessed with a book.

They went to women in a transition house in Naples, Florida, a halfway house in Gainesville, Florida, a women's safe shelter in Clay County, Florida, a few different women's shelters in northeastern Ohio, and to the women of a Salvation Army Bible Study in northeastern Florida.

My mistake provided one hundred women with the opportunity to read about someone else like them who found hope.

Further, people have since sponsored copies for women in shelters in Pittsburgh, Pennsylvania, Raleigh, North Carolina, and Jacksonville, Florida. Other ministries have purchased some to give as needed, including a family counselor in northeastern Ohio.

Considering I once viewed my whole life as a big embarrassing mistake to keep secret, I'd say God has redeemed the mess I'd made of my life.

I've heard people say, "your mess is your message" and "your test is your testimony" and I guess it's true. Giving your broken heart to God will result in wonderful things that must be shared.

Here is something else to think about before you write for publication. Do you have any bitterness or unforgiveness about your subject matter? If you do, write and write fervently. However, don't share it just yet. Writing can be healing, but it shouldn't be about bashing someone.

Pray and ask God to help you with unforgiveness. Let that scar heal thoroughly before sharing your story with others. Once you can look objectively at the entire situation, presenting it in a healthy way, then you are ready to let others into your world; to help others grow and learn from your experiences.

Here are some editors recommended on Word Weavers International facebook page:

- https://marymarvella.wordpress.com/
- http://kristenstieffel.com/
- https://thechristianpen.com/
- https://christianeditorsnetwork.com/
- https://www.christianeditor.com/
- https://www.seriouswriter.com
- https://www.bluesparked.com/
- https://christydistler.com/

Writing a Memoir

Several times I've been invited to share a workshop on writing a memoir. The first time I was asked to do so was long before I completed my own. I was a freelance reporter at a local weekly newspaper here in Florida and the administrative assistant at the Salvation Army asked if I'd come to talk to their church's Ladies Home League about writing their stories. I agreed to do it and set out to learn something about the topic on which someone thought I was an authority. That's how God works, by the way.

Dominick, my father-in-law, had written two memoirs. They weren't fancy; just for family; printed at the local print shop. He wrote the first when he was 85 and the second four years later.

Writing about your life preserves your family history. Your descendants deserve to know.

I scoured the internet for advice on the topic. I read authors' blogs, how-to articles, and even attorneys' thoughts on the legal ins and outs of sharing your personal story. I sent Dominick a list of questions about his writing process. Eva, my mother-in-law, penned the answers as he spoke.

Moving forward I referred to the seminar as "our workshop" and would report to him whenever I presented it.

I shared my findings in the class and had the Salvation Army ladies take fifteen minutes to write about a specific period of time, event, or person in their lives. The result was fascinating!

One lady wrote hers as a letter to her adopted daughter. She explained the process of bringing her into their home. She included legal details as well as emotions, and conversations, and articulately shared the ultimate joy their new child added to their family. It made me a little misty-eyed, to be honest.

Dom passed away a few years later and the notes and his comments are precious to us.

I have since shared this workshop at assisted living centers. My heart has nearly exploded seeing those treasured people write descriptions of their long lives. Wars, illnesses, losses, moves, jobs, acquaintances, relationships—they are walking history books. Their families must learn about their heritage!

I still check in, but these days I whisper heavenward. "Dom! I did our workshop again today!" And I believe he smiles at me.

Using my seminar notes, let me share a few things that I teach.

Write your memoirs for your family; to honor someone who has made a difference in your life or the lives of others. Write to heal wounds, record family history, show how you overcame adversity to encourage others, leave a legacy to future generations, or give as a keepsake or a gift. Chronicle a time in history for your family such as the weather of 2004-2005 or September 11, 2001. Document your heart and brain responses.

First, think about when. Do you want to write about an event such as following a dream, a battle with a disease, a divorce, or when you developed a philosophy? Do you want to write about a season such as motherhood or climbing a career ladder?

You may begin with an outline to help you stay on track. Break it down into one-year chunks and list the stories you want to tell: major world happenings, personal challenges and triumphs, or important people.

Envision each occurrence first. "Watch" it; live it in your mind.

Make sure your background information is correct. Research books, maps, websites, etc. Wikipedia is not a reliable source because anyone can write it. If you start there, check other sources to concur.

A fun way to gather facts is by making it a family affair. Prior to a planned family gathering, tell everyone that you want to write the family history.

Before they get there, write a one-page abbreviated family tree with a few memory-jogging questions. Paste in some clipart or family photos, and print it out on brightly-colored paper. When everyone is present, pass out the papers and ask for volunteers to help. Set your next meeting date! Assign tasks. Designate relatives from Dad's side with basic responsibilities; do the same with Mom's side.

Everyone can add their favorite anecdote. What were the person's most cherished traits; what lessons were learned from them, etc. When you picture the person in your mind, what do you see? Tell all the stories—good and bad.

Gather stories, and create a cover and page layout. You can have copies of the book printed at your local print shop. The time working together to gather this information is cherished.

Maybe you prefer to write by yourself. You don't have to write a book; you can write an essay. Just choose a theme. You may start with a list of categories. Once you've decided what you want to write about, limit yourself to 15 minutes per question. Set a timer.

Here are some categories of possible topics to consider:

My Beginnings; Challenges; Education; Emotions; Employment; Family; Favorites; Firsts; Hobbies & Interests; Homes; Marriage; Military Service; Opinions; Place in History; Relationships; Significant Events; Special Occasions; Spirituality; Talents; Traditions; Travels.

Imagine your audience first and then write to them; write so they can relate. Be yourself and write in the first person.

Keep an outline handy to remain on track. Tell both the positive and the negative. Don't tell "just the facts ma'am" but write about how you felt.

Be gracious when writing about others. Do your best to get it right—research. Write from your heart and be honest—don't write what you think you should write. Write tight—don't ramble; don't babble on; make your point and move on. Don't stereotype people. Be descriptive, not boring.

Avoid long, run-on sentences and shorten overly-long paragraphs. Start each chapter with a hook to make it engaging. Don't repeat yourself. Have a specific conclusion. Close each chapter with a question, an "Aha!" sentence, or a lesson learned. Bring it to a satisfying conclusion or lead into the next chapter.

Include quotes or statistics, stating your source. Use slang, but don't overuse it. Brief flashbacks can tie in a past event without interrupting the pace of the story.

If someone's memories are different from yours, record that, too. Probe as deeply as you can to fill out a scene or occurrence. Look at photos, diaries, letters, interviews, and background research to explain, reflect, and fill out your narrative.

An important scene needs details so the reader can experience it, but dwelling on specific elements can slow it down too much.

Use MS Word's corrections for spelling only as the grammar function is often wrong. Grammarly is a good website to help with editing and it's free. Just upload your document there and follow the prompts. Choose which suggestions you accept and delete the ones you know are wrong. Other self-editing websites include ProWritingAir and Hemingway editor, but Hemingway isn't free.

You may need to explain things you write such as slang terms or pop culture references for future generations to understand.

You DO have something important to say. Write every day. Preserve your memoir in a book or bound pages.

Pass the skills/habit of writing along. Have your kids and grandkids write down their memories when they are young. For example, ask them to write about their first day of school. Write for them if they can't yet write. It's important to ask them how they felt. You can make it a game by giving them fun prompts when writing. Buy them colorful writing tablets, books, pens, and pencils.

Writer's Block is being unable to come up with anything. Why? Possibly you're too tired to concentrate. Schedule time to write during your high-energy times. Maybe you can't write because you're stuck on a boring part. No problem. Move on to a more exciting section.

Maybe you feel your idea is underdeveloped. Go over your memories again and check the background in history books, the internet, etc.

Maybe you just feel you'd rather do something else. Tough it out; this is important. If you have restless feet and seat, just sit and write!

Perhaps you aren't confident finishing that section. Leave it and work on the one you're excited about.

Develop a routine; do what it takes to concentrate. Play specific music; take the phone off the hook.

You MUST believe that this is one of the most important things you will ever do!

Choices

There are so many choices to make as a writer. What genre? What publishing avenue? What company on that avenue?

For articles as well as books, you'll need to learn to write a query letter. This introduction to your submission should be short, reflect your writing style, and be compelling enough to make the recipient want to see your article or book proposal. There are numerous websites with instructions on how to write a successful query.

There are countless books on the craft of writing. There are online courses and individual lessons, but I've learned much from my friend Shari McGriff. Shari is an English professor and Book Coach. At the time of this writing, her school, TheWritersAcademy.net offers courses and other writing resources. I invite you to visit her website and listen to her podcast: Write Into Your High Calling.

Another helpful expert is Dianne E. Butts. Check out all she has to offer at Dianneebutts.com. From there you can find writing courses, her newsletter, and other resources.

If you write a manuscript, you will eventually need to present a book proposal to an agent or editor. If an agent agrees to represent you, he/she will help with the final proposal based on each publisher's criteria. It can take as long to perfect a proposal as it did to write the book. (I don't mean twenty years.) Please don't be discouraged. The better the final product, the better chance you have of someone welcoming you to join their publishing house.

You will need to grow your "platform." In the past, agents and publishers wanted to see large numbers of followers on social media. The last I heard, they are more concerned about how many people subscribe to your newsletter or how many you have on your mailing list. Remember research is your best friend.

If you're writing a book, you might want to learn about street teams, advance reader copies, release parties, and such. Many successful authors have blogs and articles on these topics. Even if you choose to publish independently, these are important to look into.

I don't want to sound like Captain Obvious here, but, to reiterate: Publishing has changed and traditional houses are publishing fewer authors each year. If you have a big name and a large platform they will be more willing to invest in you. If you have a topic that is attractive to them, they might take a risk on you.

Because many houses work exclusively through agents, securing that relationship is usually the first step. The best way to speak with agents and have them see your work is to attend a writers' conference.

There are many wonderful symposiums across America. To find a good fit, read reviews from previous attendees before you spend your money. Explore who will speak and what their workshops are. I've learned so much at these events.

Other considerations when choosing a writer's convention are; will the workshops offered help you grow and/or make important connections? Which agencies and pub houses will be represented? Are they looking for what you have written? Will there be opportunities to chat with their representatives? When you meet with a publishing house rep, you can sidestep an agent. It's like the fast pass at amusement parks. However, some authors advise getting one anyway because the agency can represent you in a business you are unfamiliar with. Finding an agency will be much easier once you have an offer on your book.

Where will you stay? Can you afford to stay "where the people are" or will you be off-site? Will there be opportunities for you to mingle with other writers? Some conferences offer scholarships. Don't be too proud to apply for one. It's an investment and you want to do your homework before committing.

Meanwhile, many good authors are self-publishing or partnering with hybrid publishers. I was at a writers' convention and a well-known author said, after having many books traditionally published by reputable houses, he chose to publish independently moving forward. He said doing so gave him more freedom to write what he wanted and more control over his work. Because traditional distribution takes time, he also found he could release more books on his own. Certainly, he was able to keep the publishing rights and more of the money.

If he could make that decision, I feel pretty good about independent publishing, as well.

Still, I've read so many poorly-written self-published books that I understand why some don't approve of going it alone. Always have your work professionally edited and formatted. Choose a quality cover designer, as well.

By now you are like a toy car that has been pulled back again and again. You're ready to be set free to zoom into your destiny! You have a story to share and it's time to put your thoughts onto paper.

Recognizing the restrictive lies that have held you back is the release that permits you to rocket forward. You are creative and you can write.

Find your voice and practice, practice, practice to hone your skills. That is how you will build a solid structure on your prepared foundation.

For years I wrote church and school newsletters. While serving as Salvation Army Women's Auxiliary chaplain, I wrote and presented devotionals for the monthly meetings. All these things I considered regular practice.

Don't be too hard on yourself. No one is perfect. Don't lose your unique voice by falling to the temptation to be what you believe is expected; what you think is marketable.

An editor of a large publication contacted me to write an article. He told me what they were looking for and, in my excitement to be part of their magazine, I tried to modify my story to fit his guidelines. I failed miserably.

He responded harshly in an email. "Your article rambles and repeats" was followed by some suggested topics to focus on. "Just write your own story," he concluded.

After years of writing rejection, I had developed broad shoulders and thick skin, but this shook me. His words resurrected those old lies of insecurity and failure. I nearly lost my well-fought-for tough-writer mindset.

I replied later that day that I had processed his comments and would write about one of his suggested subjects. I asked him for the deadline. I didn't show my uncertainty; I kept it professional.

Taking a deep breath, I remembered that I write for God, not for that snarky young man. I did what I'd done thousands of times. I dropped my head, folded my hands in my lap, and asked God for inspiration.

"I can do nothing, God. Anything good I have to offer comes from You. Please tell me what to write. I can't do this alone. I need You to tell me what to say."

Placing my fingers on the keyboard, I started typing and it poured out. The editor liked it, accepted it, printed it, and I got paid.

He later apologized for his insensitive words. Remember, it takes time to be kind and he was in a hurry.

Don't try to be someone you're not. Pray for God's guidance. Have faith in His perfect timing. Write in your own voice and trust the process. Hold nothing back!

Writing Conferences

Writers' Conferences are fun, intense, exhausting, and exciting to plan for. Because they are expensive, you must do your homework to choose the ones that are the best fit for you and your writing projects. Research and plan to attend as many as you feel practical.

Plan to arrive during the registration time, get signed in, get your packet of information and room assignment, and give yourself a few minutes to relax. Usually, the events begin in the afternoon or evening of registration.

Then you're drinking from the fire hose and running on caffeine and adrenaline.

There may be a social gathering so you can get to know your fellow conferees. You will have meals together and, hopefully, get to chat with the workshop leaders. There will be general sessions and even roundtable discussions where several specialists discuss a specific topic. You will be able to choose from a variety of workshops. Part of your pre-event homework will be to research the leaders of those break-out sessions. What publishing house does he/she represent? Does the company produce your genre? That way you can make sure you are attending the ones most beneficial to you and your project.

Often you will have an opportunity during the event to schedule a few minutes to pitch your project or chat with agents, publishing house representatives, successful authors, etc.

I have attended conferences at rustic camps, high-end hotels, and everything in between. It's the same everywhere. Some folks are there to learn. Some are there to shout about their successes, whether actual or not. Some appreciate authentic friendship and camaraderie. Some attendees have never published a line. Some have a cache of titles to their credit. Some have no higher education and others are PhDs in their chosen profession. You will no doubt fit in.

I've had the pleasure of speaking with publishing house representatives who were humble and kind. Unfortunately, others can make you cry. At one conference, my friend walked away from the female publishing house rep in tears. That was the same rep I was scheduled to speak with later.

At the time I was looking for an agent to represent me or a publishing house interested in my memoir. One representative was kind and encouraged me. He loved my second-choice title (the one I ended up using) and assured me I would have to self-publish.

I pulled my chair up to the woman who had made my friend cry. I smiled and handed her the introduction and the first three chapters of my manuscript, as requested. She glanced over the first two pages and said, "Have you ever read a book?" I laughed because I thought she was joking. Adults don't talk to one another that way. Certainly, Christians don't talk to each other that way. She glared into my laughing face, which was now turning crimson. I sputtered, "What?"

"Have you ever even read a memoir? THIS isn't how memoirs are supposed to look!" When I realized she was serious, I tried to keep my jaw from bumping into the table.

"Well, you're looking at the introduction. The first three chapters are behind it."

She dismissed me and I wobbled away before my five minutes were up. My friend was outside the door, talking with another writer who had been equally wounded by this insensitive representative's caustic words.

It happens. Just pull up your big kid pants and carry on. For every nasty authority there, there are probably five nice ones.

I remember my first writers' conference. It was 2001 and I was so excited! I had written a gardening devotional and hoped someone would be interested in it. I bought several weed puller tools at the dollar store. I printed out little tags with my book title and personal information and affixed them with raffia onto the wooden handles of the steel two-pronged gardening gadgets. I hadn't considered that the flight rules had just changed because of the September 11, 2001 tragedies. No one flying would be able to take that metal poker with them in their carry-on luggage!

Looking forward to the event, I squealed with excitement. It was combined with the International Christian Retail Show in Orlando, Florida, three hours from my home.

The organization I belonged to had prepared me for everything. Their registration packet had articles and guidelines. I could talk with agents and editors. This was it!

I perused the list of representatives scheduled and investigated the ones that would be a good fit for my book idea.

The paperwork said I should have digital and hard copies of my book proposal. Check. I should have a 30-second pitch ready – check. Business cards – check.

Now for my wardrobe. "First impressions count," said the guidelines. I packed my new silk skirt, gray sweater, and matching shoes. Check, oh my goodness CHECK; I was stylin'!

Hotel reservations were made, and I mapped out my days. Sunday featured a service at the convention center. Since it was on International Drive, I decided to take the "I-Ride" – a trolley that traveled "I-Drive." Transportation – check.

Armed with cover letters, a complete proposal, and an accompanying diskette (remember those?), and of course a gardening tool, for everyone I thought would be interested in my manuscript, my new messenger bag hung heavy with nearly two reams of paper. I was ready to go. I kissed Jerry goodbye and off I drove to Orlando.

Sunday morning I rode the trolley to the convention center hotel. It was a beautiful morning so I walked to the convention center next door for the worship service. It was much farther than I thought and my bag of proposals felt more like small trees. By the time I arrived, my feet were bleeding from my cute shoes.

The service was inspiring and the music angelic.

"Ignore your feet; this is going to be a good day!" Staying positive, I hobbled back to the writers' conference.

We were greeted by the organization's leaders and the instructions began. "Do NOT approach publishers while you are at the convention! This is for bookstore owners; it is NOT about you!"

That's alright, I thought. *I'm going to get to talk to them individually.*

"Do NOT give the representatives your book proposal; they have no room for extra papers!"

How many trees died for this ton of papers I'm carrying? Well, no problem; I have disks.

"Do NOT give them your proposals on disks unless they ask for them; they have more important things on their minds than you and your projects!"

My jaw dropped.

"You will NOT be able to see every publisher or agent you may want to see!"

Why am I here?

My confidence waned as what was spoken was opposite the instructions they had sent to me.

After the morning meetings were over, I returned to the main event. Soon my feet were bleeding again.

Once there, I was overwhelmed by the crowds, lines, and displays. I felt so stupid.

By now my self-assurance was gone. Unprepared for what I was facing, I couldn't get out of there fast enough. Crying, I called Jerry.

"I have no business being here."

He was calm. "We've spent so much money getting you there. Can you give it another day? Can you just go tomorrow and see what happens?" Reluctantly, I agreed. He spent the night praying.

I missed the trolley back to my hotel and fell while running for a bus. I could hear the passengers laughing. As I got on I tried to put my crumpled dollar into a slot made for tickets. The patient driver guided my money into the correct container. I stumbled and fell into a seat. An elderly woman asked if I was new in town. I guess it was pretty obvious I was a rube.

Missing my stop, I got off and walked back to my hotel.

It began to sprinkle and then pour. Carrying my three-ton bag, purse, and umbrella, I tried to keep my silk skirt dry. I reached the hotel exhausted and shoved through the wet, wiry shrubbery. "Skirt be darned!"

I wasn't leaving again. I looked at the mixture of unsalted peanuts and dark chocolate chips, the beef jerky, and bottles of water. I sighed. "Looks like dinner to me."

Sitting on the edge of the tub soaking my torn-up feet, I talked to God. "God, I'm a middle-aged, middle-class suburban housewife; what am I doing here?" I pictured myself falling by the bus. "I'm so humiliated, Lord" I whispered.

"You mean like the humiliation that causes humility?" I knew it was my Lord speaking into my heart. Somewhere I must have passed over that fine line between self-confidence and pride.

The next day I drove to the meeting and my husband's prayers were being answered.

At lunch, I met Suzanne, who I learned was from my area. We discussed our book projects, but I didn't tell her how defeated and misplaced I felt.

She told me about her first year at this function. She'd come as "prepared" as I was. She had called her husband crying, saying that she felt like she was in over her head. Her feet bled from her shoes. He reminded her that they'd spent a lot of money to get her there and asked if she would give it another day. I had goosebumps now!

She said that on her second day, she visited the huge arena where all the publishing house booths were, wearing her bedroom slippers which were plush old ladies with cigars hanging out of their mouths. That had ignited great conversations for her.

She said that this year she'd called ahead and made appointments with publishers. "I'm a big girl; I can do it myself." She had three appointments that day.

I learned great lessons that year. First, I learned to do my homework and not depend on the directions given to me. I learned to start with a good pair of shoes and build outfits from there.

I learned I should never take anything for granted. I had fantasized that I'd come looking sharp, put my proposal into the hands of publishers and agents, and have a book deal by the end of the week. Such scenarios are exceptions to the rule.

I also learned that even though I may not feel arrogant, if I don't keep my attitude in check, God will humble me. I'd left the hotel room that morning feeling on top of the world but returned with bloodied feet firmly grounded and the weight of the situation literally making me stumble.

Most importantly, I learned to never discount the power of prayer. I was put together with my wardrobe, proposals, and 30-second pitch, but I hadn't prayed. I had completely disregarded the spiritual influence of such events. Prayer is every bit as important as packing the right pair of shoes!

We learn as we go. Let's openly share how we reached our successes and what mistakes to avoid. We are here to help one another. Don't be afraid to move forward. It takes courage to take that first step, but you can do it.

If you've given your life to God and He is calling you to write, you can confidently put your writing journey into His hands.

As Dr. Martin Luther King, Jr. said, "Faith is taking the first step even when you don't see the whole staircase."

The Best Choice You Will Ever Make

If you don't understand what I mean about asking God to help you clear those rocks of doubt away; if you feel your foundation isn't properly prepared for the weight of communicating what He has put on your heart, let me explain.

For years I made terrible choices—all filtered through the lie that I had no value. The rebellion grew in my spirit and my family and I suffered from the results of my mistakes.

Terrible choices; mistakes – just palatable words to describe what the Bible calls sin.

Then I made the best decision ever. I asked Jesus to live in my heart. I asked Him to take control and be Lord over every part of my life. Not just the parts I felt I couldn't control, but every part. I asked Him to forgive me for all the bad choices—sins—I'd made throughout my life.

You see, I found out that God loves us so unconditionally that He sent His only son, Jesus, to be born as a human baby on this earth so we can relate to Him. You know, that's what we celebrate at Christmas. He grew to be a man, was crucified on a cross, put in a tomb, and arose three days later. That's what we celebrate at Easter. And He lives now in heaven and in the hearts of everyone who asks Him to come into their hearts to live.

The Bible says we ALL have made bad choices. Every person who has ever lived has fallen short of God's best for them! When Jesus died on the cross, it was His choice; no one forced Him to do it. The Bible says that that's how God showed His love for us—that while we were still sinners, Christ chose to die for us. The Bible also says that if we'll confess with our mouths and believe in our hearts, we will be saved—you know, be made whole or complete.

That was the beginning for me. God has never let me down. I've not always liked His answers. I've not always understood, or liked, His plan, but ultimately, He's never let me face a challenge alone.

Stepping down and giving Jesus total control was tough. However, it's wonderful to be God's child and obey what He says through the Holy Bible, even though it's not always easy. He has never left me and it's awesome to know I never have to face another tomorrow without Him.

For further details, please visit the "Make a Positive Change" tab on my website, kellystigliano.com.

As promised, this book isn't exhaustive. It's just one lady's path to publication and some of the mistakes made along the way. I hope you've been able to glean some helpful ideas and guidance through this writing.

I invite you to watch for future "How Did You . . ." editions!

Acknowledgments

Because I am nothing without Christ, I thank Him first and foremost. Any good idea I have comes from Him. When I get ahead of myself, He slows me down. I can do nothing successfully without Him.

Even before my mother suspected my existence, God knew me. For those few weeks when I was a secret from humanity, He communed with me. Although I don't remember this, it makes me feel special. God's plan for my life would not be thwarted by anyone or anything, seen or unseen. Twists, detours, and interruptions could not upset His map for my life. Thank You, Father, Son, and Holy Spirit!

A special thank you goes to my parents who made me go to school even when I didn't want to. Although some would say my hyperactivity kept me from excelling, here I am with many anthologies and two originals completed. Together you've cheered me on in my writing journey and now Dad cheers me on from heaven. You're both the best and I'm blessed to be your daughter!

I'd like to thank my children who encourage me to write. From school newsletters to magazine articles to books, you've always believed in me. Your support means so much!

Thank you, sweet Jerry, for putting up with late dinners, a messy house, and a disheveled wife. When I threw on sweats and slippers and shuffled toward my computer you said, "Dressed for success, I see." Your humor keeps me going! You support my writing, listen to draft after draft, and gently nudge me to keep going when I get distracted. Your input is important. I will cherish you always!

A special thank you to Shari McGriff for your writing classes. They, and you personally, have brought me back on track the countless times I've lost focus. Your support means so much to me!

Thank you to my fellow Word Weavers for critiquing the chapters I've shared. Your input is invaluable! Special thank you to Victoria Roberts for helping me pull the weeds in the back-cover blurb.

Thank you to my beta readers. Please know your time and discerning eyes are so appreciated. Your comments help keep me in line. You are important!

Thank you to the people who have asked me about how I got started writing. You see something in me that I don't. When I feel like a failure, you see me as a success. I thank God for you. This book is for each of you. Now get writing! **You have a story that only you can tell!**